CW01638014

Dad's GREAT ADVICE®: Top Ten Greatest Great Advice of All Time

Other Dad's Great Advice Books available at greatadvicegroup.com

Dad's Great Advice for Teens

Dad's Great Advice for Parents of Teens

Dad's Great Advice for College Students

Dad's Great Advice for Everyone

Dad's Great Advice for All Parents

Dad's Great Advice About Life Skills for Teens

Dad's GREAT ADVICE®: Top Ten Greatest Great Advice of All Time

MARC FIENBERG

Published in the United States by Story Press
info@greatadvicegroup.com
greatadvicegroup.com

Library of Congress Control Number: 2022944547

Paperback ISBN 978-1-7351804-7-2
Ebook ISBN 978-1-7351804-8-9
Hardcover ISBN 978-1-7351804-9-6

Printed in the United States of America

First Edition

For the top ten (or more) greatest people in my life: My family and close friends.

Contents

The Best of the Best

Everybody has some advice to give… but it ain't always good advice!

Over the years, I've spoken with and interviewed lots of dads, moms, therapists, psychologists, businesspeople, economists, entrepreneurs, and other experts, and I've read lots of the most interesting scientific studies and research. I've collected advice from people all over the world, and I've cataloged it so that I could more easily identify the pieces of advice that were the most valuable to most people, advice that you might refer to as… Great Advice.

I've collected Great Advice that's valuable to many different groups of people, at many different stages of life, and organized that advice into books for some of these groups, most notably teens, college kids, and parents. Thousands of people have read the books in the *Dad's Great Advice* book series over the years, and as you might expect, I've received quite a bit of feedback from people about that Great Advice, especially the particular piece of Great Advice that each person "voted for" as their favorite.

Everybody had different reasons for voting for the Great Advice that they chose. Some cast their vote for the piece of Great Advice that they thought was most important to them, some voted for the one that they felt was most insightful, and others voted for the one that was most unique or interesting to them.

I tabulated all the votes, compiled a list of the most popular pieces of Great Advice from all the *Dad's Great Advice* books, and placed all of that Great Advice together in one place: this book! It's not just Great Advice—it's the crème de la crème of Great Advice! The Super Bowl of Great Advice! The best of the best Great Advice! It's...

Dad's Great Advice: Top Ten Greatest Great Advice of All Time!

The Great Advice listed in this book will help you:

- **Become More Successful**
- **Develop Loving Relationships**
- **Get Healthier**
- **Live Life to the Fullest**
- **Manage Time Better**
- **Reach Your Goals**
- **Take Smart Risks**
- **Build Strong Connections with Others**
- **Empathize with Others**
- **Maintain a Positive Attitude**
- **Improve Your Confidence and Self-Esteem**
- **Find Happiness**

If you're looking for help in any of the areas above, then I'm confident that reading *Dad's Great Advice: Top Ten Greatest Great Advice of All Time* will be well worth your time!

Enjoy the book,

Marc

A Warning About Great Advice

Reading about Great Advice isn't really all that valuable if you don't eventually put some of that Great Advice to use. In other words…

Don't just read this book. Try to live it.

But I must warn you: It can be overwhelming to try to put all the Great Advice in this book, or even just some of it, into effect. Reading about Great Advice is easy, but putting even one of these pieces of Great Advice into effect is hard. Really hard. The good news is that I've developed something that can help you.

For each piece of Great Advice in this book, I developed a short checklist of a few simple challenges that will help you put the Great Advice into effect. This "Challenge Checklist" includes some simple tasks you can do (usually in less than five minutes) to immediately see the benefits of putting the Great Advice to work for you. Some of the challenges are difficult, some are easy, some are scary, and some are simply thought-provoking.

The *Dad's Great Advice: Top Ten Greatest Great Advice of All Time: Challenge Checklist* is included with the purchase of this book, and you can download it for free here:

greatadvicegroup.com/checklist10

If you want to get the most value out of this book, and want a bit of help in translating the Great Advice into action, please make sure to download the free *Challenge Checklist* to help you get started.

Dad's Great Advice:
Top Ten Greatest Great Advice of All Time #10

(From *Dad's Great Advice for Everyone #1*)

Figure Out How to Be Successful

Figure out for yourself what it means to be successful, and remember that the things that make other people feel successful might not be the same things that make you feel successful.

If I were to ask you who the most successful people in the world are, what names first come to mind? The most popular answers I get to this question are Bill Gates, Jeff Bezos, and Warren Buffett.

Why do those people keep coming up more than any other? After all, there are lots of successful business people in the world who have built really successful companies that are helping lots of people live better lives. So why those three? The answer is probably obvious: money.

Those three people happen to be among the richest people in the world. They're at the top of the top of what we call "the 1 percent." And the way most people measure somebody's success is by how much money they have.

Here's the interesting thing though. If you're making more than about $32,000 a year, you are part of the 1 percent too. To be specific, you're part of the top 1 percent of income earners in the world. That means you're earning more than eight billion other people. So does this make you feel successful? And if you're not making more than $32,000 a year, does that make you feel unsuccessful?

Maybe. Maybe not. But regardless, is money the only way of measuring success? Is money the best way of measuring success?

No, it isn't.

In fact, the best metric to measure success is not the amount of money you have, but rather, it's the amount of happiness you have. Happiness is the one thing we're all trying to maximize. Now it just so happens that most people believe the biggest driver of their happiness is how much money they have. But is it actually true that money really does drive happiness?

As it turns out, it isn't true. Money is not the biggest driver of happiness. Not by a longshot.

In the most recent rankings of the richest countries of the world, Qatar was ranked the highest in per capita income. But you may be surprised to learn that Qatar is only ranked 29th when it comes to happiness. On the other hand, Finland is ranked all the way down at number 24 when it comes to average per capita income. But Finland is also ranked as the happiest country in the world. So why isn't the richest country the happiest, and why isn't the happiest country the richest? (And more curiously, why is Finland so happy when they're also so cold?)

Even though most people directly tie money to happiness and success, when they are pressed on the issue, most of them quickly realize this isn't true. Don't believe me? I'm going to make you a deal, and I'd like to know if you would accept the offer.

I'll snap my fingers and make you an instant billionaire. You will have all the money you will ever need, a beautiful house, a huge yacht, a private jet, and most importantly, the latest iPhone. But... in the process, you'll lose contact with all your current friends, your spouse or significant other, your parents, your brothers and sisters, and your extended family members. You'll have all the money you want but you'll have no loved ones to share it with. Is that success to you?

I'm guessing it's not. And I'm guessing it's not because I happen to know that a lot of people who have a huge bank account, a huge house, and a huge yacht, also have huge therapy bills. And they have huge therapy bills because they realized, perhaps a bit too late, that their success wasn't only driven by money, and that they may have dropped the ball in other areas of their life in which they also measure their success and happiness.

There are lots of other ways to define success, other than how much money you have. One of the best illustrations of this I've heard is a story that my good friend Archimedes Clutterbuck told me the last time he went skiing. He took a lesson with a ski instructor who had been doing his job more than forty years. The instructor lived a pretty spartan, frugal life, living out of his van most of the year. But he also told Archimedes, "I'd rather live out of my van and ski every day out in nature than make ten times more money and be stuck inside at a desk all day." He measured his success not by how much money was in his bank account, or how big a house he lived in, but by how many days a year he was able to ski.

The things that make your friends think you're successful, the things that make your parents think you're successful, and the things that make your colleagues think you're successful, might not be the same things that make YOU feel successful. You're responsible for figuring out for yourself the things that will make you feel successful and the things that will bring you happiness.

And there are a huge variety of things that you might use to determine how successful you are: how many days you get to ski, how many close friends you have, how many people you make laugh, how many kids you have, how many countries you visit, how much time you spend with your significant other, how many lives you save, how many trees you plant, or how many people you feed.

So don't assume that money is the best measure of your success and happiness, because it probably isn't. Figure out for yourself what it means for you to be successful.

"Don't measure your success with someone else's ruler."

–Unknown

Dad's Great Advice: Top Ten Greatest Great Advice of All Time #9

(From *Dad's Great Advice for College Students #4*)

Don't Have Too Many Friends

Don't worry so much about how many friends you have. When it comes to friendship, it's all about quality, not quantity.

In our society, it seems like we're taught that more is always better. More money, more cars, more possessions, more power, more status, more everything! Obviously though, it's not exactly true, or even close to true. One area in particular that this rule doesn't apply is when it comes to friendships.

With friendships, more does not mean better.

Lots of people aspire to be popular. Popular people have plenty of friends and admirers who want to spend time with them. It's like being a bit of a local celebrity. And as a result, people often go out of their way to accumulate a lot of friends. Even our social media tracks how many "friends" or "followers" we have, even though most of them can't really be considered friends at all, just acquaintances. Or even strangers.

Creating new friendships is obviously a really good thing to do. And it seems like the more friendships we create, the better. Especially in college, where the opportunities to meet new people and create friendships are ten times more abundant than what you experience in the "real world," you might naturally have the tendency to be so overwhelmed and excited by all the new people you meet, that you end up trying to maintain every single one of those friendships. In short, you feel like you want to be friends with everyone you meet.

But there's a big problem with having a lot of friends. You end up spreading yourself really, really thin. It takes a lot of time and effort to keep up with friendships, and the more friendships you try to keep up with, the more time and effort it takes. As a result, you end up with lots and lots of friends, but no close friends.

And close friends are what life is all about. Close friends are the ultimate goal.

Close friends are something more than just a friend. So much more. They make you a better person. They support you when times get tough. They listen to you. They're honest with you (whether you're right or wrong). They always have your back (whether you're right or wrong). They make you laugh. They make you feel better. They help you live longer. They help you chill out. They keep you humble. They forgive you. They trust you. They truly care about you.

It's not easy to find a close friend. In fact, if you're lucky enough to find even two or three close friends in your lifetime, I think you're doing pretty darn well. It's a challenge to find a close friend primarily because of all the time it takes to find someone you really connect with, and to build enough trust with them to move the friendship to the next level.

In fact, scientists have studied friendship and figured out about how long it takes to develop a friend and a close friend. Short answer: a lot of time. They found that It takes, on average, 164 hours of time together for an acquaintance to become a friend. And to make a good friend, it takes, on average, spending 219 hours together! So obviously, the more people you're acquaintances or friends with, the harder it is to spend the 219 hours it takes to really connect and bond to create a "close friend."

I should be clear that having some close friends still doesn't preclude you from having lots of other friends. The key is to make sure that you're spending extra time—quality, meaningful time--with your close friends. Because if you're trying to connect closely with too many people at once, you end up not connecting closely with anybody at all. In other words, finding and developing close friends is a matter of depth over breadth. Quality over quantity.

Don't worry so much about how many friends you have. Focus on developing your relationships with your close friends by spending quality time with them.

"Wishing to be friends is quick work, but friendship is a slow ripening fruit."

–Aristotle

Dad's Great Advice: Top Ten Greatest Great Advice of All Time #8

(From *Dad's Great Advice for Teens #3*)

Spend Your 44 Hours Wisely

Spend your free time on the things that will bring you lasting happiness, not just things that are fun in the moment.

"I don't have time for that."

I hear it all the time, from teens and adults alike. But *really?* You don't have time for "that," whatever "that" is?

Allow me to convince you otherwise.

I'm not great at math, but with 24 hours in a day, and 7 days in a week, that gives you 168 hours to spend as you please every single week of every single month of every single year of your life. This is true regardless of your race, religion, sexual orientation, where you live, how much money you have, what country you come from, how smart you are, how pretty you are, or how nice you may be. Time is the great equalizer; we are all given the same amount of time each week no matter what our lot is in life.

Sadly, if you're one of those human beings that need to sleep every night, then you lose a bunch of those 168 hours. But even after accounting for eight hours of sleep a night (if you're lucky), that leaves you with 112 hours each week.

"But school!" you say. "What about school?"

Even after accounting for eight hours of school every weekday, that leaves you with 72 hours each week.

"Yeah, but I've got homework. Soccer practice. Lots of chores. And my memes! I love memes! I gotta have time to look at my memes!"

Even after accounting for four hours a day of some mandatory obligations you have to take care of, and of course, those all-important memes, that leaves 44 hours each week.

And 44 hours every week is A LOT of time.

All of this makes the statement, "I don't have time for that," a little hard to believe. While you have the physical need to sleep, and an obligation to go to school and do homework, you have control over how you prioritize and spend those remaining 44 hours in your week. So rather than saying, "I don't have time for that," a better, more accurate statement would be, "I don't want to spend my time doing that." That at least acknowledges that you have control over how you prioritize spending your 44 hours. And once you realize that you do have control over how you spend your 44 hours, make sure you spend them wisely.

Keep track of how you're spending your 44 hours, because what you'll find is that, day by day, week by week, year by year, those hours will slip away from you.

You'll spend those hours on things that are easy to spend them on, the most common one being consuming television, videos, or social media. It's relaxing. It's enjoyable. And it's easy, so why not? You deserve some downtime, don't you?

You do! But keep track of how much downtime you give yourself. The average teenager spends about three hours watching television each day. That brings your 44 hours down to 23. And the average teenager also spends about three hours on social media each day. Sadly, that leaves you with just two measly hours each week.

So how are you supposed to spend your 44 hours? How are you

supposed to think about your 44? It's not easy, but I've found that the best way to think about how you want to spend your 44 hours is by separating them into two main categories: "Today Me" hours and "Tomorrow Me" hours.

Today Me hours are hours you spend making yourself happy now—relaxing or enjoying the moment, giving you instant short-term gratification. They are hours spent on things like watching videos, consuming social media, napping, and of course, looking at memes!

Tomorrow Me hours are hours you spend that might not be quite as relaxing or enjoyable in the moment (although they can be), but that will make you happy over the long term, for weeks, months, years, or a lifetime. They are hours you spend doing things like studying for an algebra test, practicing the guitar, or learning how to create your own memes!

Today Me hours make Today Me pretty darn happy, but kind of upset Tomorrow Me, who never really gets to enjoy those hours. Tomorrow Me hours frustrate Today Me, who could be having a much better time, but make lots of Tomorrow Me's happy.

There's room for both types of hours in your day—things you do just to enjoy the moment and recharge your batteries, and things you do that are a bit of an investment for future enjoyment. It's obviously very easy to spend your Today Me hours, but a bit more effort and discipline is required to spend Tomorrow Me hours. If you need help motivating yourself to spend Tomorrow Me hours, just try to remind Today Me that, even though they might not be so happy right now, Tomorrow Me is going to be really grateful and happy for the Tomorrow Me hours you're spending today.

Keep track of how many of your 44 you are spending on Today Me hours, watching something, looking at someone else's creations, relaxing, bringing yourself instant gratification and enjoyment, but no meaningful benefit once the television show or YouTube video is over. And keep track of how many of your 44 you are spending on Tomorrow Me hours, helping you learn something, create something, connect with somebody, reach your goals, become a better person, or assist somebody else in becoming a better person.

Forty-four hours a week, every week of the year, every year of your life, leaves you LOTS of time outside of sleep, school, and homework to do other things. Use that time wisely, on things that will bring you lasting happiness, and even though Today Me won't have quite as much fun, Tomorrow Me will thank you.

"The chief cause of failure and unhappiness is trading what you want most for what you want right now."

–Zig Ziglar

Dad's Great Advice: Top Ten Greatest Great Advice of All Time #7

(From *Dad's Great Advice for Teens #9*)

Step Into the Arena

Get out of your comfort zone and take risks in life.

Teens get embarrassed. A lot. I mean A LOT. I'm guessing you're embarrassed just reading this and knowing that I'm addressing you directly, right?

You probably care a lot about what your friends and acquaintances and family think about you. You probably even care about what crazy Aunt Edna thinks about you. And naturally, because you don't enjoy being embarrassed, you tend to try to minimize the amount of embarrassment you experience. That's to be expected. But it's such a shame.

It's a shame because one of the main side effects of trying to minimize the amount of embarrassment you experience is playing it safe. And playing it safe is an awful way to live your life—especially when you're a teen and the stakes of not playing it safe are so low.

Yes, yes, I fully appreciate the enormous risk you're taking by leaving the house with your hair looking like that (great mohawk, by the way). I understand that your life will be over if people ever hear what a terrible karaoke singer you are. I know that you will be ostracized from your community if anyone learns that you've been to seven Justin Bieber concerts (and perhaps you should be ostracized).

We all understand that the stakes are pretty high for a teen, and the risks you are sometimes tempted to take are big ones. But I have to let you in on a secret: When you compare these risks to some of the risks you'll be taking when you're an adult, they pale in comparison. And so…

Learn to take risks. Learn to take lots of risks. Now. While you don't have much to lose. And let me assure you that, if you don't have a spouse or kids to take care of, and if you do have parents that are around to support you emotionally and financially, then you really do not have much to lose.

Try out for the cross-country team! I know, if you do, you risk the embarrassment of being the slowest person on the team, and having to hang your head in shame each time you come in last place, and endure the taunts of everyone on the team calling you "The Tortoise." But if you don't try out for the team, play it safe, and sit on the sidelines, you risk the silent torture of watching everyone else enjoy the thrill of competition week after week, and wondering if you could have beaten them all if only you had just taken a risk.

Raise your hand in class when the teacher asks a tough question! I know, if you do, you risk a few moments of shame when you answer "The Battle of Gettysburg" when the question your math teacher asked was, "What is the square root of forty-nine?" But if you remain silent and don't raise your hand, you risk letting another student answer the question, giving the exact same answer that you would've given, and hearing the accolades of the teacher saying to somebody else, "So impressive that you knew that answer!"

Take it from President Teddy Roosevelt, the eight-time winner of the prestigious "best presidential mustache" award, who said (paraphrasing), "The people who criticize others do not count.

The credit belongs to the person who steps into the arena, whose face is marred by dust and sweat and blood, who tries valiantly, and who, at best, knows the triumph of winning, and at worst, fails while daring greatly. That person never has to worry about being one of those frightened critics who doesn't ever win or lose because they never even tried."

As good ol' Teddy says, step into the arena! As long as the risks you take are not dangerous or irreparable, take those risks! Don't sit on the sidelines when you could be in the arena playing the game. Being in the arena is exhilarating. Being in the arena is exciting. Being in the arena is fun. Being in the arena means you have the chance to experience all of that, and win big. Being in the arena means that, even if you lose, you had an amazing experience, became stronger in the process, and did more than every other person sitting on the sidelines, watching you compete in the arena.

Step into the arena. Take some risks.

"Take risks. If you win, you will be happy. If you lose, you will be wise."

–Unknown

Dad's Great Advice: Top Ten Greatest Great Advice of All Time #6

(From *Dad's Great Advice About Life Skills for Teens #7*)

Set Formal Goals

Writing down and tracking your goals might be one of the most valuable life skills you ever learn.

I'm sure you have goals in your life. They might be big goals, like becoming a talented architect one day, or small goals, like beating the final boss in your favorite video game. If you're like most people, you spend a bit of time worrying about whether or not you're going to reach those goals.

What if I told you there was something you could do that would make it 42% more likely that you would reach your goal? I'm guessing you might reply that you don't want to expend all the extra time and effort it would take, even if it really were to increase your chances of reaching your goal by 42%. Fair enough.

But what if I told you that it would take you less than twenty seconds? Now would you do it?

It's not a joke. Science has shown that there's something you can do in less than twenty seconds that really will increase your chances of reaching your goal by 42%. All you have to do is simply…

Write down your goal.

So go ahead and write down one of your goals! I'll wait.

I know it seems crazy, but the simple act of writing your goals down increases your chances of achieving those goals for a bunch of reasons. The act of writing them down forces you to more clearly define exactly what it is you want to accomplish, it subtly motivates you more to work toward your goal, and it causes you to strategize about what your plan should be to attack your goal.

Writing down well-defined goals also helps in a lot of other areas, including self-confidence, responsibility, time management, resilience, perseverance, and developing a growth mindset.

Unfortunately, the opposite is also true. Without having any well-defined goals, you might find that your life simply becomes a thoughtless process of living one day to the next, without knowing where you're trying to get to or what you're trying to do over the long term.

So take some time to formalize the short-term and long-term goals you have, simply by writing them down. It's worth the time, and it's easy to do.

And if you're willing to write down your goals, maybe you're willing to take the next step and set better-defined goals in a more structured way. In fact, here's the crash course in how to do that in a super easy and fast way:

Crash Course in Goal-Setting

1. Write down one of your long-term goals.
2. Break down your long-term goal into smaller, shorter-term, more easily attainable sub-goals. Each sub-goal should be small enough that it can be accomplished in about a week.
3. Spend the week achieving that sub-goal.
4. Celebrate that you just got one week closer to your long-term goal!
5. Check in on your next sub-goal, and work toward that.
6. Repeat over and over until you get to the end of the long-term goal.

Congratulations! You just graduated from the Dad's Great Advice School of Goal-Setting. That's one less goal you have to achieve now.

And now, if you're interested in earning your advanced degree in goal-setting to get it just right, keep reading to learn about a more organized, methodical way.

Advanced Course in Goal-Setting

1. **Core Values**

   Start your goal-setting by… ignoring your goals completely and listing out your core values, the very high-level things you care most about in the world that should drive your goals. Try to limit your core values to the five that are most important to you. If you focus on too many core values, then you end up prioritizing none of them.

   There are lots of different core values that might be important to you, but here are some ideas you can choose from:

   - Family, friendship, success, beauty, happiness, money, security, love, health, altruism, fame, creativity, status, honesty, kindness, leadership, accomplishment, intelligence, recognition, justice, respect, wisdom, fun.

2. **Long-Term Goals**

   Write down some of the long-term goals you have. By "long-term" I mean goals you have that might take you ten to fifteen years to accomplish. These should be really big, lofty goals. Don't give too much thought to how realistic your long-term goals are, because almost any goal is realistic if you give yourself ten to fifteen years to achieve it. Plus, as you may learn one day, there are lots of people in this world who are going to try to convince you to give up on your goals and dreams, so the last thing you want to do is join in and quash your own goals just because it's going to take a lot of time and hard work to get there. What if a six-year-old Lionel Messi didn't set goals for himself in soccer because it was too unrealistic to become a professional soccer player?

If you need help figuring out what some of your long-term goals are, ask yourself these questions:

- What would you do if success was guaranteed?
- What does the life you envision for yourself fifteen years from now look like?
- What challenges do you face that, if you overcame them, would make you really proud?

Come up with one to three long-term goals in each of the following areas of your life:

- Work/Career
- Home/Family life
- Community/Society
- Self

Here are some examples of long-term goals:

"In fifteen years from now, I want to..."

- (Work/Career) Be a senior research biologist developing better vaccines
- (Home/Family Life) Be married with two children
- (Community/Society) Be a volunteer teacher at my local school
- (Self) Weigh 140 pounds and become a black-belt in karate

Whenever possible, make sure that your goals are as well-defined and as measurable as possible. For example, making your goal "Become a black-belt in karate" is better than "Get better at karate," and "Be a senior research biologist developing better vaccines" is better than "Be a scientist who helps discover things."

Once you choose your goals, write down the purpose of each goal, or why you chose that specific thing as your goal. Remembering the "why" behind each goal of yours helps keep you focused on your motivation toward that goal. Most purposes should include how that particular goal helps or serves other people in society, but if your goal doesn't happen to help other people, that's OK too.

EXAMPLES:

- I want to be a biologist so I can help discover a cure for an illness/condition.
- I want to volunteer as a teacher so I can help young kids get excited about learning new things.

Lastly, cross-reference your long-term goals with the core values you came up with earlier, and make sure that your goals match up with your core values. For example, if one of your core values is "Family" but one of your long-term goals in the Home/Family Life area is "Live alone in the wilderness for seven years," you might want to ask yourself if that is really the right goal for you, or conversely, if that really is one of your core values. There's nothing worse than working towards a goal for fifteen years only to figure out once you've achieved that goal that it's not really something you care about deep down inside.

3. **Short-Term Goals**
   There's one big problem with having long-term goals set for ten to fifteen years from now: Those long-term goals aren't really that helpful in figuring out what you need to do on a daily, weekly, and monthly basis to reach them. But fear not. That's why we've got… short-term goals!

   Take each of your long-term goals, and break those goals into smaller and smaller short-term goals. First, determine a realistic sub-goal of your long-term goal that you could realistically reach within the next year. Then once you have that year-long goal, break that down further into sub-goals you can accomplish in the first three months, the first month, and the first week.

   For example, if your long-term goal is to become a black-belt in karate, a good goal for the next year might be to get your yellow belt in karate. Over the next month, as you work toward your yellow belt, a good goal might be to learn your first two karate forms. And over the next week, a good goal might be to learn the first two parts of the first karate form.

   Again, make sure your short-term goals are as specific and measurable as possible, so it's absolutely clear if you achieved a goal or not. "Getting better" at karate is not a very measurable goal, and it will be hard to know the exact moment you achieve it. But "earning a yellow belt" is a very measurable goal, and you'll know you've achieved it the moment they place that yellow belt in your hands.

4. **Track Your Goals on a Regular Basis**
   This could be the most important part of goal-setting. If you set a goal for yourself to achieve something by next year, but you don't think about that goal again until next

year, there's a pretty good chance you're not going to reach that goal. Instead, put regular "goal check-ins" on your calendar to make sure you're making progress toward your yearly goal by achieving your quarterly, monthly, and weekly goals.

These check-ins don't need to take more than a minute or two. But make sure that you take time each week to remind yourself of your goal for the next week, and that you take time each month to remind yourself of the goal for the next month, etc.

Most importantly, when you do achieve one of your short-term goals, celebrate the small win! Because it's the small wins of achieving your goal for the week that keep you motivated and eventually add up to achieving your goal for the year.

I'll be honest with you: there are a lot of adults who go an entire lifetime without ever setting formal goals for themselves. And some of them probably reach some of their goals anyway. But everybody has goals they're trying to reach, and if the science is clear that the more formalized you are about setting and tracking your goals, the more likely you are to reach those goals, why wouldn't you spend the time to learn that skill and do it?

Writing down and tracking your goals might be one of the most valuable life skills you ever learn.

"People with goals succeed because they know where they're going."

–Earl Nightingale

Dad's Great Advice: Top Ten Greatest Great Advice of All Time #5

(From *Dad's Great Advice for Parents of Teens #12*)

Promise Them Real Unconditional Love

If your teen knows that nothing they do will ever cause you to love them any less, they'll feel a lot more comfortable being themselves, or asking for help when they need it.

"I love my child unconditionally."

If you're a parent, you've hopefully uttered this phrase a time or two, and hopefully within earshot of your kid. But have you given thought to what that implies? What it truly means at its core?

It's easy to love your child when they're being your perfect little angel. But what about when they're upsetting you? Or annoying you? Or outright pissing you off? What about when they fail, or mess up, or do something that you disapprove of? What about when they do something that brings shame to your family? What about when they betray you, or steal from you, or physically hurt you? Can you still love them even then?

Before you answer, let's be clear that if we're really taking the phrase literally, "unconditional love" means that you love somebody without conditions. You love them no matter what they say or do. But unconditional love doesn't mean unconditional approval. You can reject somebody's actions without rejecting them. And so...

Are you able to disapprove of your child's actions, but still love your child?

I believe the answer to that question for every parent should be… Yes. Every child deserves unconditional love from their parents. And every parent should be able to love their child even while they disapprove of the actions their child has taken.

Because the alternative to unconditional love is… conditional love. A love for your child that is conditioned upon them earning your love by doing a certain thing, or being a certain person, or saying a certain thing, or acting a certain way, or accomplishing a certain thing. If your child has to go through life with the constant pressure of knowing they need to earn your love by acting in a certain way, they're never able to feel the freedom to be the person they truly want to be. And that's a pretty crappy way to have to live your life.

Every human being deserves the security of knowing that, even if everything else in their life goes wrong, there will always be at least two people who love them, regardless of whether those people approve of the actions their child takes, or the choices their child makes, or the person their child becomes.

If you agree, make that promise to your teen. Promise to love them unconditionally. To love them truly without conditions. No matter what. No exceptions.

Make sure they know that they don't have to (and can't) earn your love by doing something, saying something, being someone, or acting a certain way. Make sure they know that you will always love them, not because of what they do, or who they've become, but simply because they're your child.

Unconditional love means you love them even when they piss you off, even when they get bad grades, even when they dent your car, even when they get suspended from school, even when they say they hate you, and even when they vape. Unconditional love means you love them even when they get arrested, even when they pursue a career you disapprove of, even when they steal from you, even when they lie to you, even when they love somebody you disapprove of, even when they embarrass you, and even when they let you down over and over.

Unconditional love does not mean that you give your teen anything they want and set no boundaries for them. Unconditional love does not mean you don't discipline them and punish them. Unconditional love does not mean that you never get irritated by them, or feel like you want to kick them out of the house, or actually kick them out of the house if that's what's best.

It's perfectly natural and human to be annoyed with or irritated by your teen from time to time, or even most of the time. And you might even find that there are times when you don't want to be around them, or when you don't even really like them all that much. If you happen to have those feelings, you're in good company with lots of other parents. The key thing to remember is that, regardless of what anger or annoyance or irritability you feel with your teen, you make it clear that they are still loved.

Unconditional love for someone means that even when you don't like them, you still love them.

No. Matter. What.

"But how can I make it clear that I still love them when I can barely stand to be in the same room with them?"

It's actually not hard at all. One of the simpler ways of making sure your teen knows you love them is to always finish each day with a reminder of your unconditional love. For instance, let's say you get in a huge fight with your teenager, and unkind words are spoken by them (something about comparing you to a guy named Satan). Tensions are high. You and your teen have each taken a few hours to calm down, but you're still getting the silent treatment. And yet, on your way up to bed, you kiss them on the forehead (or at least try to before they violently pull away from you) and tell them, "I love you." You probably get absolutely no reaction.

And yet, they get the message. They know. They know that, even though you're angry with them, and they're angry with you, they are still unconditionally loved, and always will be.

Have a hard and fast rule that, no matter what happens during the day, right before you turn in for the night, you kiss your teen and tell them, "I love you." Even if you have to grit your teeth while you say it. No exceptions.

Is it sometimes hard to remember that you love your teen when you're in the middle of an enormous disagreement? Sure. But the stakes are pretty high.

My good friend Archimedes Clutterbuck loved his daughter, Cleopatra Clutterbuck, unconditionally and told her so many times. But when she turned fifteen and wanted to tell her father that she was gay and was dating another girl, she was worried. She knew Archie had some pretty strong cultural and religious beliefs against homosexuality, and she was worried that he would never speak to her again. In fact, she was so worried that she considered just trying to act heterosexual for the rest of her life despite what she felt deep down inside, at the core of her being. That would've been a disaster, a truly awful way to live.

When Cleo finally worked up the nerve to tell him, Archimedes wasn't happy about it, and wasn't really able to hide it from her. He admitted to her, "It's not the life I want for you, and it's not a lifestyle that I approve of." And yet, moments later, when the tears were done flowing, Archie kissed his daughter on the cheek and told her, "I still love you, and I always want you to be happy."

It probably wasn't the best reaction possible, but he certainly did make sure Cleo knew that, even though he didn't support her lifestyle, he still loved her unconditionally.

(And fortunately, although it didn't happen overnight, Archie eventually did come around to fully embracing both his daughter's lifestyle and her partner, and is now quite a vocal advocate for LGBTQ+ issues!)

Archimedes' story is pertinent not just for parents of LGBTQ+ children, but all parents, because there's not one parent out there whose expectations and hopes and dreams for their child ever matched up perfectly with reality. It's just that some expectations end up farther from reality than others. Regardless, it all comes down to this:

Even when they do something you disagree with or don't approve of, love your child.

If you want your teen to be secure with themselves and feel comfortable pursuing the things that are really at their core, you'll learn to love your teen unconditionally, and make sure they know that they truly are loved unconditionally.

A teen who truly knows that they have the unconditional love and acceptance of their parent, no matter who they become or what they do, is much more likely to feel secure enough to become the person they were meant to become, whether it's a person who identifies as gay or queer, a person who converts to a different religion, a person who pursues an unexpected career, a person who is gender non-conforming, a person who marries somebody much different from themselves, or a person who simply acts in a way that is counter to their parent's wishes.

Similarly, a teen who knows that they have the unconditional love and acceptance of their parent, no matter what mistakes they make or trouble they get into, is much more likely to feel secure enough to come to you for help when they need it, whether it's a teen who gambles too much, a teen who becomes addicted to drugs, a teen who steals, or even a teen who commits a crime that lands them in prison.

Knowing they will always have unconditional love from their parent is one particularly important foundational thing that every teen needs to help them make it through the teen years and beyond.

Give absolute acceptance of whoever your child turns out to

be, or wants to be, even if it's somebody you wouldn't normally accept. If your teen knows that nothing they do will ever cause you to love them any less, they'll feel a lot more comfortable being themselves, or asking for help when they need it.

"These six words can save your child so much unnecessary pain: 'I love you as you are.'"

–Scott Barry Kaufman

DAD'S GREAT ADVICE: TOP TEN GREATEST GREAT ADVICE OF ALL TIME #4

(From *Dad's Great Advice for All Parents #5*)

TEACH THEM A GROWTH MINDSET

Teach your child to develop a growth mindset, which will help them realize that they're able to learn almost anything they set their mind to.

Not so many years ago, if your young kid did something wrong, the most common way to punish them was to undo your belt and use it to whack their butt until they cried. What better way to teach somebody not to do something than with the punishment of pain!

These days, most of us have come to the conclusion that beating our child is a bit counterproductive and cruel, and doing so will typically get you thrown in a jail cell. It's just one example of how, every now and then, humankind takes a big leap forward and discovers something that we were doing wrong all along.

One of the most recent big leaps forward in parenting came more than a decade ago from a Stanford psychologist named Carol Dweck, who described a new theory of intelligence around kids who develop a "growth mindset" versus a "fixed mindset." The theory has become so popular and influential that it's not just applicable toward parenting your children, but it's now used with adults and even in corporate settings. It's a big enough deal that it should be one of the main things you focus on as your child develops.

The fixed vs. growth mindset simply deals with two different ways of thinking about where our abilities, talents, and intelligence come from.

The fixed mindset approach is the old-school way of thinking, and it states that everybody is born with innate strengths and weaknesses that are "fixed" and unchangeable. For example, it taught that some people are "just not good at math," and once you discover this, you should avoid math and instead focus on something else that you are naturally good at.

On the other hand, a growth mindset teaches that abilities, talents, and intelligence can be learned and improved upon with enough effort and persistence. It teaches that our success and the things we are able to achieve are largely (although not entirely) within our control, not something fixed that we're either born or not born with. To be clear, having a growth mindset doesn't mean that with enough effort anybody can become a Nobel-prize-winning genius or a professional athlete (and my own experience playing little league baseball proves this), but rather, that people can improve upon themselves if they work at it. As it turns out, adapting this growth mindset of having some control over your own destiny plays a huge role in a person's success and anxiety level over their lifetime. As a result, it's a pretty powerful habit that can make a huge difference in your kid's life (and your own!).

So is it possible to teach our kids to develop a growth mindset, or is it just one of those things that your kid is either born with or not?

That was a trick question! If you're thinking with a growth mindset, then you already know that it's possible to teach your kids to develop a growth mindset. It does take a little work, though. There are lots of different strategies you can use to teach your kids to develop a growth mindset (and to develop a growth mindset of your own along the way). So many strategies, in fact, that I've detailed them out into their own separate pieces of Great Advice that follow. But here's a quick summary:

- Use language that reinforces a growth mindset
- Find appropriate challenges for your kid
- Encourage perseverance
- Celebrate your kid's failures

Teach your child to develop a growth mindset, which will help them realize that they're able to learn almost anything they set their mind to.

"Everything is hard before it is easy."

–Johann Wolfgang von Goethe

Dad's Great Advice: Top Ten Greatest Great Advice of All Time #3

(From *Dad's Great Advice for Everyone #2*)

Take the Miracle Drug of Our Time

This miracle drug has so many amazing benefits that you'd be crazy not to take it.

If you spend any time on the internet, then you've probably seen your share of advertisements for vitamins or supplements. "Live longer!" they say. "Control your weight!" they claim. "Improve your sex life!" they promise. And "all for a low, low price if you act right now!" of course.

Everybody seems to have a vitamin or supplement they're shilling. Some of them are legitimate, but many of them are just sugar pills sold by snake oil salespeople making crazy health claims that have absolutely no basis in science. You should be very skeptical of anybody selling a miracle drug that promises amazing health benefits.

Except for me.

Because I have a miracle drug that really does deliver amazing health benefits! And I'll sell it to you for a low, low price! But you have to act now!

I normally don't try to push vitamins or supplements on people, because it's just not clear who needs them, which ones really make a difference, and what the side effects are of each one. And yet, the miracle drug that I push happens to be the one and only medicine out there that science actually has done enough research on, and it's one that I feel comfortable staking my reputation on and recommending wholeheartedly.

It's not a multivitamin, it's not fish oil, it's not a probiotic, and it's not a protein powder. Those things may or may not be worthwhile to some people, but none of them pack the punch of this miracle drug.

I call it a miracle drug because, while some vitamins and supplements help improve one or two aspects of your life, mine improves your life in many, many ways all at once. There's not one prescription or over-the-counter drug that improves your life in as many different ways as my miracle drug. Don't believe me? There are multiple scientific, peer-reviewed studies that prove my miracle drug can help you:

- Feel happier
- Increase your energy and productivity levels
- Improve your brain function, focus, and memory
- Reduce stress, anxiety, and depression
- Improve your relaxation and sleep quality
- Increase creativity
- Control your weight
- Quit smoking
- Improve your self-confidence
- Strengthen your muscles and bones
- Improve the look of your skin
- Lower your risk of heart disease, cancer, and diabetes
- Reduce chronic pain
- Live longer
- Improve your sex life

But wait, there's more!

Over the past several years, my miracle drug has quickly become the number one doctor-recommended drug, and luckily, you don't need a prescription for it.

But wait, there's more!

It's not expensive at all! In fact, if you're resourceful, you can probably get it for free!

My miracle drug may be one of the best-kept secrets out there, because only 20% of people actually take my supplement. Why do so few people take advantage of such a powerful medicine? The only reason I can think of is that my miracle drug has one very tiny, minor drawback: it's one of those rare medicines that's not yet available in pill form, so it's not quite as convenient to take. Still, it only requires a simple, painless treatment, done a few times per week, that you can safely and easily self-administer in your own home in just ten to thirty minutes.

So what is this miracle drug that is doing so much for so many people so inexpensively? It's called…

Exercise.

I know. You think I was misleading you by describing exercise as a medicine, or a supplement, or a drug. But I wasn't. Doctors and scientists now agree that the health benefits of exercise are so wide-ranging, so convincing, and most importantly, so effective, that they are now "prescribing" exercise to their patients as medicine. In fact, if exercise were a pill, it would have a trillion dollars in sales, and would be prescribed to everybody. That's how powerful and effective it is.

I wasn't kidding when I mentioned all the benefits of this miracle drug. There are scientific studies that show evidence of each of the health claims outlined above. We've known about some of the benefits of exercise for a long time, and nobody even disputes some of the more common claims, such as the fact that exercise helps control your weight, gives you more energy, reduces stress, and strengthens your muscles and bones. However, we've now come to believe that exercise helps improve other areas of our lives that most people are surprised to learn about, such as the fact that exercise improves your brain function, makes you feel happier, increases creativity, and helps you sleep better. And of course, once it becomes common knowledge that exercise improves your sex life, we're likely to see a lot more people at the gym.

And yet, even though exercise works as a miracle drug by improving our lives in so many different ways, only 20% of the population actually exercises. If you're part of that 20% that is already exercising three to five times a week, then give yourself a pat on the back (which should be easier to do because of the extra energy and stronger muscles and bones that exercise has provided you!).

If you're part of the 80% of the population that doesn't regularly exercise yet, it's time to get with the program! Say "no" to drugs, but say "yes" to *this* drug.

There's really no reason not to exercise anymore. Would your life be better if you experienced some of the benefits of exercise listed above? Yes! So if exercise would improve your life in so many ways, why the hell aren't you exercising?!

"I don't have the time to exercise."

Well, what if exercise didn't take that much time? If you actually could take exercise in pill form, and experience all the benefits of exercise without any side effects, you'd be crazy not to, right? After all, it takes just a minute to walk to the medicine cabinet, open a bottle, pop a pill into your mouth, and wash it down with some water.

As you may already know, exercise is not yet offered in pill form. But what if I could promise you all the benefits of exercise in just twenty minutes? Would twenty minutes be fast enough?

In fact, many studies show that just twenty minutes of exercise three times a week will bring you most of the benefits associated with exercise. Sure, that's nineteen minutes longer to exercise than to take a pill, but aren't those nineteen extra minutes worth it to get all those benefits? No? That's still too much time for you?

Fine, you drive a hard bargain. Spend just five minutes a day exercising, because there is some evidence that shows that just five minutes of intense exercise can get you some of the benefits of exercise! And even the busiest people in the world can find five minutes in their day, especially if it's likely to make the rest of their day so much better.

"All right, I have the time. I just don't have the money to join a gym."

Ancient Roman gladiators were in pretty good shape, and I hear they didn't have much access to fancy elliptical machines or treadmills. You don't need a gym to exercise! And even if you did, no matter what city or town you live in, there's an amazingly inexpensive gym right near your home: the great outdoors. And, unlike those other gyms, this one is open 24/7 and smells a lot better!

Even when it's that time of year when the great outdoors gym is a bit too cold or too hot for your taste, there's yet another gym that's just as convenient and just as inexpensive: your home gym. Just search the internet for "home workout videos" and you'll find tons of ways to get some exercise without ever leaving home.

"Fine, I don't need to spend money to exercise. But I'm still not doing it, because it's just too painful!"

It's true, exercise can be painful when you really push yourself hard, and your heart begins to pound, and your muscles start to burn, and you can't catch your breath. That's not a great feeling for most people. However, I have a simple solution that will make exercise a completely pain-free experience for you: just take it easy! Don't push yourself so hard!

Nobody said that when you exercise you have to try to compete with world-class bodybuilders or marathon runners. If your muscles burn too much when you're lifting twenty-pound barbells, try ten-pound barbells instead. If your lungs feel like they're going to explode when you run, don't run. Walk! The days of personal trainers screaming at you to lift more weight and push yourself to the edge of exhaustion are over. You can still get many of the benefits of exercise without getting anywhere near the point where it causes you pain.

"Yes, I suppose I could take it easy when I exercise. But I'm still not doing it, because it's just too darn boring."

Exercise as a whole isn't too boring, it's just that the exercise you've chosen to do is too boring. You need to choose a different, more interesting way to exercise.

I'm willing to bet that there's at least one method of exercising out there that you'll find fun; you just have to figure out what it is. Some of the more obvious methods of getting some fun exercise are running, biking, swimming, or playing competitive sports.

But if those options don't light your fire, some of the less-obvious (but just as good!) methods of getting some exercise are walking, dancing, rock climbing, rollerblading, hiking, jumping rope, hula hooping, kickboxing, cleaning the house, skiing, trampolining, bowling, walking your dog, moving furniture, hitting at a batting cage, snowshoeing, boxing, golfing, or kayaking.

Heck, even if you're 100% couch potato, you can still get some exercise simply by playing video games using a virtual reality headset.

We're all looking for ways to improve our lives and be happier, but it's often really hard to find ways to get the benefits quickly and effectively. Exercise happens to be one method of improving your life and becoming happier that is 100% within your control; it's easy to do, and you'll start seeing the benefits almost immediately. Stop making excuses, and start exercising right away. This miracle drug has so many amazing benefits that you'd be crazy not to take it.

"The hardest thing about exercise is to start doing it. Once you are doing exercise regularly, the hardest thing is to stop it."

–Erin Gray

Dad's Great Advice: Top Ten Greatest Great Advice of All Time #2

(From *Dad's Great Advice for College Students #18*)

Have Deep, Meaningful Conversations

The building blocks of creating close friendships are deep, meaningful conversations, so have as many of those conversations as possible.

Hopefully, I've already convinced you of the value in developing a few really close friends in your life. But that's easier said than done, isn't it? Finding a really close friend is something that is likely to happen only a handful of times in your life. It's rare to meet somebody you really click with. So how do you improve your chances or accelerate your meaningful friendships?

Well, I'm happy to report that if you're living on a college campus, especially if you're living in a dorm, you're in the perfect position to do just that.

Obviously, college already has a lot of things going for it: learning about interesting new things, living on your own for the first time, being challenged in ways you've never been challenged before, and of course, going deep into debt while paying obscenely high tuition prices. (OK, maybe that last one isn't so great.)

But one of the most valuable things that college has going for it is it's probably the first (and perhaps the last) time in your life when you are surrounded by an entire microcosm of people your age–fascinating and interesting people with completely different and diverse backgrounds, beliefs, and interests. Especially if you live in a dorm, most of your time is spent surrounded by your peers, without an adult in sight. Living in close quarters with so many young people creates an amazing environment to have some pretty special shared experiences. And those shared experiences typically cause some really close friendships to develop. And that is probably one of the most valuable things that college has going for it. Those shared experiences with friends. And those shared experiences with friends are exactly what turns close friendships at college into lifelong friendships throughout life.

These valuable shared experiences can be any number of different things. It might be going to school football games together, or acting crazy at a party together, or sneaking into a bar with fake IDs together, or eating your meals together in a dining hall, or simply watching your favorite TV show together. But one of the most valuable shared experiences you could possibly have at college also happens to be one of the simplest: just having a deep, meaningful conversation with other people.

Why are deep conversations so important and valuable? Science has actually studied this very question, and has proven that deep, meaningful conversations are strongly tied to happiness. They're tied to happiness for two main reasons. First, we human beings seem to be complicated creatures, and one of our most basic drives is to create meaning in our lives. Having meaningful conversations helps us do just that. Second, we human beings also seem to be very social creatures (even the introverts among us), and deep conversations help us to connect with others.

In fact, I mentioned earlier that scientists have found that you need to spend an average of 219 hours with another person to turn a friend into a truly close friend. However, those same scientists have figured out a sneaky way to artificially shorten the time it takes to develop a close friend: by having deep, meaningful conversations.

Deep conversations can take on many forms, and can be about many different topics. They can be about topics you all agree upon or topics you violently disagree on. Deep conversations can be about topics that make you uncomfortable or topics that you've discussed many times before. The only real requirement for a deep, meaningful conversation is that the topic is… deep and meaningful.

"This is some weather we're having, huh?" doesn't really help get you to the meaningful stuff. "What are your hopes and dreams in life?" gets you closer. "Why are those your hopes and dreams?" probably does the trick.

It's pretty easy to create deep, meaningful conversations with somebody, but here are a couple tricks to help you along the way:

- Be genuinely interested in learning more about the human being sitting across from you. That's generally enough to get a deep conversation going. Be inquisitive about things you never knew about them.
- Look for topics that you disagree on, but rather than becoming combative and trying to convince them of your point of view, probe and challenge them to find out why it is exactly that they hold that specific opinion. Try to be open-minded to their point of view, and ask how they'd respond to counterarguments.
- Ask personal questions, and volunteer your own personal thoughts and feelings as well. This requires a lot of vulnerability, but it will increase the amount of trust you build with somebody quickly.
- While somebody is telling you something interesting, focus less on how you're going to respond when they're done talking, and more on the substance of what it is they're saying. Long awkward pauses in a

deep, meaningful conversation aren't really awkward at all, but rather an indication that things are deep and meaningful.

- Prepare a list of deep, meaningful conversation topics. There are entire books written just focused on deep, interesting questions, and ten times as many lists on the internet with similar conversation starters. Here are my favorite questions used by those scientists who found that deep conversations accelerate close friendships:
    - If you could choose anybody in the world as your dinner guest, who would it be?
    - For what in your life do you feel most grateful?
    - If you could change anything about the way you were raised, what would it be?
    - Is there something that you've dreamed of doing for a long time? Why haven't you done it?
    - What are your most treasured and your most terrible memories?
    - When did you last cry?
    - What does friendship mean to you?

Some of your most memorable times in college will be some of the amazing, deep, meaningful conversations you have with others sitting on the floor of your dorm room, or at a restaurant at one in the morning, or walking to class across the entire campus.

Deep, meaningful conversations will become the building blocks of some of your closest friendships throughout your life. So do what you can to have as many deep, meaningful conversations as possible.

"Good conversation is as stimulating as black coffee, and just as hard to sleep after."

–Anne Morrow Lindbergh

Dad's Great Advice: Top Ten Greatest Great Advice of All Time #1

(From *Dad's Great Advice for Teens #2*)

Don't Make Your Parents Happy

Be your own person, and make yourself happy, not your parents, because all they want is for you to be happy anyway.

As humans, we look to other people for approval and validation sometimes. You probably look to your friends, teachers, social media followers, and others to see how "cool" your clothes, jokes, friends, hair, grades, makeup, shoes, and other things are. (Your hair looks great, by the way. I love what you've done with it!)

If you've ever posted anything to Instagram and checked every three minutes for the next twelve hours to see how many "likes" you received, then you know what I'm talking about. But if you're like most teens, of all the people you're looking to for approval, on the very top of that list is... your parents.

Teenagers are known for going out of their way to drive their parents crazy. After all, that's really your primary job as a teen, right? Ironically, you probably also spend a lot of energy trying to make your parents happy and proud of you.

You should know though, teens who expend a lot of effort to make their parents happy and proud of them turn into adults who expend a lot of effort to make their parents happy and proud of them. And a lot of those adults spend a large portion of their lives, sometimes their entire lives, continuing to expend a lot of effort to make their parents proud of them, sometimes even after their parents are dead and gone. (And trust me, it's not easy to make somebody proud once they're dead.)

The industry for psychologists and therapists is about 20 billion dollars, and in my very unscientific estimate, about 19.6 billion of that is driven by people looking for help with issues in getting their parents' approval. And if you were to interview all the doctors and lawyers in the world, I'm pretty sure you'd find that about 34.8 percent of them became doctors or lawyers because their parents wanted them to.

Don't fall into this trap. Don't spend your life trying to gain the approval of your parents, or of anybody else in this world. It's hard enough to figure out what it is that YOU want out of life, and then accomplish it, let alone try to temper that with what your parents want. And it's a sure recipe for unhappiness.

My good friend Archimedes Clutterbuck wanted to be a doctor when he was in high school. Or to be more accurate, his parents wanted him to be a doctor. "But Archie," I said, "every time you give blood, you faint." Regardless, he spent four years getting a pre-med degree, then four years in medical school, then five years as a resident, and then he officially became a doctor. And when he stood up on that stage as they handed him his medical license, he looked out at his parents in the audience, smiles plastered across their faces, beaming with pride. His parents took him out to a celebratory dinner, bought him a fancy desert, gave him a fancy stethoscope as a gift, and then… they went home. And Archimedes was left standing there… as a doctor. Going to work… as a doctor. Being… a doctor. Every day. For the rest of his life. (Fortunately, Archie soon quit his job as a doctor, and was ten times happier as a result.)

Now put yourself in Archie's shoes. Imagine you don't really want to be a doctor, but you spent thirteen years studying to be a doctor just to make your parents proud. Imagine that you have a lifetime ahead of you, doing something every day that you don't really want to do. Imagine that every day of your life, you'll be making your parents really happy, but not yourself. And chances are, if you're like most people who find themselves in this situation, you'll become more and more miserable day after day, week after week, month after month, year after year. But on the plus side, at least your parents will be happy, right?

Wrong.

You probably won't ever really believe this until you have children of your own, but most parents are proud of their kid regardless of what their kid does or accomplishes in life. Nothing you can do can decrease—or for that matter, increase—the amount of pride your parents have in the person that you are. Nothing you can do can increase or decrease the amount of love your parents have for you. Your parents' pride and love for you is unconditional and infinite. (If you want to prove the point, go ahead and smash grandma's antique vase and see if your parents get over it. Hint: They will. Eventually.)

When you succeed at something, that smile on your parent's face is not a look of pride; it's happiness at the pride that you probably feel about yourself. When you fail at something, that sad look on your parent's face is not a look of shame; it's sadness at the disappointment that you might feel about yourself. And strangely, sometimes when you fail at something, you might be observant enough to see a tiny gleam of a smile on your parent's face. Trust me, it's not your parent secretly experiencing a bit of schadenfreude at your failure. It's their happiness that you risked failure, and had the strength to give it your best.

In the end, your parents really only want one thing for you: happiness.

Are there exceptions to this parenting rule? Of course. A lot in fact. Many parents screw up royally. They push you in a direction that they think will make YOU happy, even though they don't realize that they're actually pushing you in a direction that will make THEM happy. Don't tell your parents I revealed this closely guarded secret, but as it turns out, many parents actually make mistakes. And this parenting mistake might even be one of the more common ones. But your job is to make sure you don't let their mistake become yours.

Regardless of what your parents want for you under the guise of making you happy, only you know what's really going to make yourself happy. Whatever that thing is, do that. Wholeheartedly. With no apologies. And no matter how hard it is for your parents in the short term, remind yourself that, in the end, if you're happy with your decision, your parents will probably realize that they're happy too. And if you're in the unfortunate situation of having parents that don't ever get to that place of happiness, it ends up being their problem, not yours.

Make sure that the path you choose in life is one you choose for your own reasons, to make yourself proud and happy, not to impress your parents, or to gain your parents' approval.

"It's important to make somebody happy, and it's important to start with yourself."

–Unknown

HONORABLE MENTIONS

Not every piece of Great Advice can be graced with the honor of a spot on the prestigious list of *The Top Ten Greatest Great Advice of All Time*! Many pieces of Great Advice came close, but fell just short of the top ten, and, as a result, I thought it was appropriate to issue some of those pieces of Great Advice an honorable mention. The following are five pieces of Great Advice that just missed out on the top ten. Enjoy!

Dad's Great Advice: Top Ten Greatest Great Advice of All Time
Honorable Mention

(From *Dad's Great Advice for Everyone #21*)

Fail on Your Way to Success

Failing to try is really the worst failure of all. So give up your fear of failing, and remember that failing is the most common path to success.

It feels great when you succeed. It kind of sucks when you fail. You would probably prefer to succeed rather than fail. I know I might be going out on a limb here, but I'm confident that's all true.

But don't worry so much about failing. I know you'd probably rather get a paper cut and pour lemon juice on it than to fail, but I'm here to convince you otherwise. (Besides, there's not much upside to getting a paper cut and pouring lemon juice on it, although I'm certain a video of you doing so would get about a billion views on YouTube).

Failure doesn't always have to be a bad thing. Failure doesn't even always have to mean that you failed. You can reframe and rethink every failure and mistake as something more positive, as just another step toward gaining more experience on your way to ultimate success.

Even more importantly, remember that, usually, failure is actually a success in disguise.

For instance, my good friend Archimedes Clutterbuck spent a lot of time and money to start a business repairing computers. He found many customers that needed their computers to be repaired, but unfortunately, he didn't have the knowledge he needed to do many of the repairs quickly, and his business eventually failed. Obviously, he wasn't so happy about that.

But in the course of that failure, he realized that, although he wasn't good at fixing computers, he was really great at finding customers that needed computer repairs. And as it turns out, there were lots of computer repair companies that needed help finding customers. So he started a new business that helps repair companies find customers, and that new business is an amazing success. And of course, he would've never realized that the market had a need for his service if he hadn't first started his repair business and failed at it. That's success disguised as failure!

But remember, failure can also be disguised as success. Imagine you set a goal to run a 5K race in less than sixty minutes, and on your very first try, you not only accomplish that goal, but you actually finish the race in thirty minutes. Congratulations! We're all very proud of you. Fantastic success!

But is that really a success? If your goal was to run the 5K in sixty minutes, and you actually ran it in thirty minutes the first time you tried, maybe you didn't set your sights high enough. Maybe running five kilometers in thirty minutes isn't such an amazing accomplishment after all. You might even say that, even though you succeeded at running a 5K race in less than an hour, maybe you failed by setting your goal so low to begin with.

Now it's certainly true that, when you set your sights really, really high, you're significantly increasing the chances that you're going to fail or make a mistake early on in the process. But that's fantastic! Don't treat it as a "failure," treat it as a sign that you've successfully challenged yourself to accomplish a lofty goal, and you've successfully discovered one way not to accomplish that goal. With every additional "successful failure," you rule out yet another wrong way of doing it and get closer and closer to finding the right way.

In fact, if you've never failed at all, that in and of itself is one of the greatest failures of all. If you've never failed at something, then you've probably only set really safe and realistic goals for yourself. You've probably never really pushed yourself. Never really challenged yourself. Never really set the bar high enough.

Or even worse, maybe you've never failed because you just don't even try. Because you'd rather not attempt something at all than risk failing at it. Because your fear of failing is stronger than your drive to succeed.

Fear of failure is a really common problem for a lot of people, and I can tell you that it's one of the saddest problems to have. It's sad because it's a paralyzing fear, keeping you from accomplishing amazing things. Fear of failure guarantees that you won't fail, but it also guarantees that you won't succeed.

So give up your fear of failing! Failing to try is really the worst failure of all. Failing is not the end of the world, but rather, the most common path to success.

"It is impossible to live without failing at something, unless you live so cautiously that you might as well not have lived at all. In which case, you fail by default."

–J.K. Rowling

Dad's Great Advice: Top Ten Greatest Great Advice of All Time

HONORABLE MENTION

(From *Dad's Great Advice for Teens #24*)

Compare Yourself to Only One Person

Comparing yourself to others is a waste of energy. The only valuable person to compare yourself to is Yesterday Me.

Most teens find themselves competing and comparing themselves constantly to those who are closest to them. For lots of teens, that means they compare themselves to their siblings, their parents, their friends, their classmates, their community, and sometimes even Jay-Z or Beyoncé.

When my good friend Archimedes Clutterbuck was a kid, he loved Trivial Pursuit. And he found that he was constantly comparing his trivia knowledge to that of his two sisters. When comparing himself to his older sister, this meant he was always falling short because of his disadvantage in age. And when comparing himself to his younger sister, this meant he was always coming out ahead because of his advantage in age. And eventually he realized the comparisons were really all just a façade.

He recognized that whether he came out ahead or behind was determined not by his actual knowledge of trivia, but by who he compared himself to. And that was somewhat arbitrary. Eventually, he decided to play it safe and just compare himself to the four-year-old girl across the street, which meant that he always came out ahead on everything.

What's the point of comparing yourself to somebody else? Is it to determine how good or bad you're doing at something? If so, that's a flawed comparison. It's less a measure of your skill, and more a measure of who you decide to compare yourself to.

There are 7.8 billion people in the world today. Why would you choose to judge yourself only in comparison to those who live in the same house as you? Or to those who are in the same classroom as you? Or to those who are in the same school as you?

Let's say that, compared to your best friend, you're the fastest at running the 100-meter dash. Congratulations! And let's say that, compared to all your classmates at school, you are still the fastest at running the 100-meter dash. You're amazing, you little speed demon!

But as you expand your comparison to different groups, eventually you'll find that you're no longer the fastest anymore, even though you're still just as fast as you were before. There might be a kid in another school district who runs faster than you, or a kid in the next county who runs faster than you, or a kid who lives in a different part of the state who runs faster than you. You don't feel so fast anymore, huh?

Unless you've won the gold medal for the 100-meter dash at the Olympics, there's always going to be somebody on this planet who runs faster than you. And on the flip side of the coin, there's always going to be somebody on the planet who runs slower than you.

Comparing yourself to others will either give you a false sense of security, or worse, give you a false sense of inferiority. And I'll give you one guess to tell me if most teenagers are more likely to compare themselves to somebody that makes them feel superior, or inferior. If you said teens are more likely to compare themselves to somebody that makes them feel superior, then you are absolutely, 100 percent… living on some other planet.

And so the point is, rather than compare yourself to somebody that's going to make you feel bad (or good) about yourself, don't waste a second comparing yourself to others at all. It's not productive, it's not informative, and it's not actionable. Most of the time, it's simply destructive.

"But if I don't ever compare myself to anybody," you might say, "then I don't have any incentive to push myself to get better." Good point! There's actually some truth to that. As a result, I suggest you make one big exception to the "no comparisons to others" rule.

The only person you actually should compare yourself to on a regular basis is somebody you should refer to as "Yesterday Me." If Yesterday Me ran the 100-meter dash in fifteen seconds, then it makes sense for Today Me to compare yourself to Yesterday Me and aim to finish in fourteen seconds. Comparing yourself to Yesterday Me makes sense, because it's the one person in the entire world for whom you know it's a fair comparison.

Otherwise, you risk thinking you're the best or worst at something, not because you actually are the best or worst at that thing, but only because you're the best or worst at something as compared to some tiny percentage of the population. And that means nothing.

Don't compare yourself to others. Just compare yourself to Yesterday Me.

"If you continuously compete with others you become bitter, but if you continuously compete with yourself you become better."

–Unknown

DAD'S GREAT ADVICE:
TOP TEN GREATEST GREAT ADVICE OF ALL TIME
HONORABLE MENTION

(From *Dad's Great Advice for Teens #4*)

DON'T BELIEVE A WORD YOUR BOYFRIEND/GIRLFRIEND SAYS

When trying to figure out how "into you" your boyfriend/girlfriend is, put more weight on what they do, than what they say.

There are many honest people in this world who say exactly what they mean and, for better or worse, will truly express how they feel about their significant other. The world needs as many of these people as possible.

And yet, there are others who are not so honest and forthright—people who are, to use a technical term, jerks.

There's a well-known stereotype out there about the male gender that goes something like this: "Guys only have one thing on their minds." Naturally, that one thing is... Taco Bell.

OK, it's *not* Taco Bell. The one thing they're referring to on every guy's mind is... sex (or any kind of sexual experience), although Taco Bell might run a close second.

Like all stereotypes, it's unfair to apply this to everyone. There are a lot of guys out there who don't have a one-track mind. And conversely, there are a lot of girls who, like some guys, only have that same thing on their minds too.

Whether a guy or a girl, having sex in their thoughts isn't, in itself, a bad thing. Every single one of the 7.8 billion people on this planet owe their existence to sex, and almost every single one of those 7.8 billion people will have some sort of sexual experience before they leave this planet. And because there are approximately 7.8 billion people having sex, whoever invented sex way back when made sure that it was a fun, enjoyable experience.

The fact that many guys and girls often seem to have sex on their mind isn't the problem. The real problem is that when sex is the only thing on somebody's mind, a person tends to say anything they need to say to convince somebody else to satisfy that amazingly strong human desire, whether it's true or not. They might say things like, "I love you so much," or "I want to be in a committed relationship and only date you," or "I really care a lot about you," when it doesn't really reflect their true feelings.

Now some people really mean it when they say those things. But some don't. So how do you know which type of person you're talking to? How can you tell the person that really means the beautiful things they say, from the person that doesn't? How can you tell the person who really cares about you from the person who really only cares about fooling around with you?

It's actually quite simple: *Don't listen to what they say; watch what they do.*

Here are some things that people DO that demonstrate they might not like you as much as you think they do:

- They say they're going to do something with you, but then cancel or don't follow through.
- They always have to have things their way, rarely giving in or compromising.
- They ask for lots of favors, but don't do many favors for you.
- They only make plans with you at the last minute, when they don't have anything else to do.

- They disrespect you by saying mean things or calling you names.
- They don't call or text you that often.
- They don't ask questions about you.
- They don't take interest in the things you're interested in.
- They don't introduce you to their friends, or don't pay attention to you when their friends are around.
- They often can't find time to be with you because they're too busy.

On the other hand, here are some things that people DO that demonstrate that they probably really like you:

- They do the things they say they're going to do.
- They often give in and compromise.
- They do favors for you when you ask.
- They make plans with you days or weeks in advance.
- They say nice things to you, and say nice things about you.
- They call and text you often.
- They ask a lot of questions about you, and about what's going on in your life.
- They take interest in the things you're interested in, even if those things don't interest them.
- They introduce you to their friends, and pay close attention to you when their friends are around.
- They try to spend a lot of time with you, even if they're busy.
- They try to do things that make you happy, and try to avoid doing things that make you unhappy.

You'll notice a common theme among most of the items above: They all take a lot of time.

Somebody that really cares about you wants to spend time with you, and wants to spend time doing things that make you happy. Somebody that doesn't really care about you, has an easy time saying nice things (which doesn't take that much time), but has difficulty spending the time that it takes to demonstrate that they really care about you.

In short, a jerk will say anything they can to get what they want, because it's quick and easy to fake. But they won't usually DO the things that show they care, because it takes a lot more time to fake that.

If you're questioning somebody's feelings for you, ignore all the things they say, and pay attention to all the things they do.

"Actions speak louder than words."

–Proverb

Dad's Great Advice: Top Ten Greatest Great Advice of All Time

HONORABLE MENTION

(From *Dad's Great Advice for Teens #14*)

Try Everything

Live life to the fullest and try everything at least once. It will change you as a person.

When you were a baby, you had a lot of "first time" experiences: The first time you rolled over, the first time you ate mashed peas, the first time you pooped mashed peas. There's a reason that some of the most viral videos are those of a baby's look of excitement while sucking on a lemon for the first time, or standing up for the first time. One of the most exciting things about being a baby, a toddler, a pre-teen, or a teenager, is the excitement of doing things for the first time, and those babies remind us how excited we used to get from experiences that now seem boring and mundane.

You're probably not that excited about sucking on a lemon or standing up anymore. (At least I hope you're not.) But there are still a lot of firsts out there for teens. There's the first time you drive, the first time you vote, the first time you kiss somebody, the first time you climb a mountain, the first time you waterski, the first time you skydive. The list is endless.

"But… it's scary," you say.

Yes! That's the whole point. It's scary to drive for the first time. It's scary to climb a mountain for the first time. It's scary to sky-dive for the first time. It is scary. And it may seem dangerous. But remember this: Almost anything you do that sounds scary and seems dangerous isn't really that dangerous if you go about doing it in a smart way. And a smart way usually means doing it for the first time with the assistance and guidance of somebody more experienced than you.

For instance, if you want to skydive, and you decide to just strap on a parachute and jump out of an airplane, perhaps you really should be scared. On the other hand, if you hire an experienced instructor to take you on a tandem skydive, with you strapped firmly to their chest, and then you go through hours and hours of training and testing before actually jumping out of an airplane on your own, your level of danger is reduced significantly.

Fear, however, is not the only thing you'll feel when you do something for the first time. You'll also feel an unparalleled excitement that quickly overpowers the fear—a flow of adrenaline coursing through your body that you don't get with many other things. And this excitement alone is reason enough to try new things that you've never done before. It contributes toward living an exciting and passionate life.

But there are lots of other reasons to try new things. For one, you're young. Too young to be set in your ways. Too young to be closing your mind to new experiences. Too young to be saying "I'm not a skydiver," or "I don't like climbing mountains." Be open to trying new things, and you'll probably find that you will experience things that change your routine, change your opinion of things, change the way you look at the world, and in general, change you in unpredictable ways.

And if nothing else, if you try something new and don't like it… well, that's one thing that you now know you don't like, and one thing that you now don't have to wonder about liking anymore.

I hope it goes without saying, but just to be clear, when I say "Try new things," I don't mean you should try absolutely everything. There are a bunch of dangerous, illegal, or immoral things that don't ever need to be tried: heroin, robbing a bank, cheating on your boyfriend/girlfriend, punching somebody. You should obviously take a pass on these things.

But if it's unlikely to hurt you, or anybody else, then do yourself a favor and try it. Just once.

Broaden your horizons! Suck the marrow out of life! Try new things! There's a really good chance you'll be happy you did.

"Twenty years from now, you will be more disappointed by the things you didn't do than by the things you did do."

–Unknown

DAD'S GREAT ADVICE: TOP TEN GREATEST GREAT ADVICE OF ALL TIME

HONORABLE MENTION

(From *Dad's Great Advice for Everyone #10*)

HELP SOMEBODY

Give some of your time to help somebody less fortunate than yourself. If you give of yourself, you will inevitably get more than you expect.

There is a Chinese proverb that says: "If you want happiness for an hour, take a nap. If you want happiness for a day, go fishing. If you want happiness for a year, inherit a fortune. If you want happiness for a lifetime, help somebody."

In this day and age, we sum up the same sentiment with the phrase, "It's better to give than to receive."

Why is everyone so generous? What are people getting from giving?

As it turns out, a lot.

Scientists have given us compelling data to support the idea that one of the best ways to happiness is by giving to others and helping others. But there are a lot of ways to give and help.

The easiest way is to give your money. You can give your money to charities, non-profits, some stranger on a street corner, religious institutions, etc. And it feels good to take money that you worked really hard for, and give it to people who need it a bit more than you do.

But you know what feels even better?

Giving your time. As you may have learned by now, your time is significantly more valuable than your money.

If you've never spent the time to volunteer in a soup kitchen, or deliver meals to the homeless, or help volunteer in the oncology ward of a hospital, or given of your time to help others on a one-on-one basis, you should. The feeling you get after donating money is significantly different than the feeling you get after personally helping people truly in need, people significantly less fortunate than yourself.

Giving your money is great. But it's quick and impersonal. Giving your time allows you to see, meet, connect with, and build relationships with the people that you're helping. Obviously, it takes a bit more effort to give your time than your money. After all, you usually can't just show up at the hospital and ask to volunteer, you have to submit an application and probably get a bit of training. But there are simpler ways to give your time.

You probably pass a homeless person on the street every once in a while, right? It only takes about ten minutes to buy two sandwiches and sit and talk to them while you share a meal. You probably live somewhere near a retirement home, right? It only takes about twenty minutes to pass out a dozen roses to the residents, listen to their stories, and brighten their day.

You don't even have to leave your house to give your time. If you search for "Virtual Volunteer" you'll find dozens of websites like onlinevolunteering.org (run by the United Nations) and dosomething.org (tailored for young people to enact social change) that enable you to help people all over the world without ever getting up from your chair.

Whatever you decide to do, giving your time to help others has a bunch of really nice byproducts.

It will make you more empathetic to other people and their situations. No matter how much you read or watch about what it's like to be homeless, you can't possibly know and feel what a homeless person goes through without getting to know them personally and hearing their story.

It will make you more grateful for what you have. Keeping up with the Joneses is a real problem in our society, and you might be one of those people who constantly compares yourself to anybody who is better off than you. But sometimes, it's good to be with people less fortunate than yourself, simply to remind yourself how silly it is to think about and be anxious about some of the "first world problems" you have.

It will make you appreciate the real drivers of happiness. When you meet people less fortunate than yourself, you might realize something surprising. Often times, you'll find that many of these "less fortunate" people seem to be significantly happier than you'd expect, given their circumstances. You might even find that many of them are significantly happier than you are.

Think hard about this. If someone who sometimes struggles to meet their basic needs, like food and shelter, has such a positive attitude, and can be so happy with so little, perhaps they know something you don't. Perhaps the things you think will make you happy are not really the things that will actually make you happy.

And let me give you some additional Great Advice to help you supercharge the feeling you get from giving: Keep it a secret. Don't tell anybody that you gave money to the charity, or volunteered at the hospital, or bought a meal for the guy on the street corner, or helped serve food at the homeless shelter. Keep this one part of your life just for yourself.

Why? When you tell people you did something generous, you get the added benefit of feeling proud that people know that you did something generous. But you'll also find that, eventually, you start questioning, "Am I really doing this to be generous, or am I doing this just because it makes me feel good to know that people think I'm a generous person?"

Don't allow yourself to question your own motives. Keeping it a secret ensures that you never have to wonder why you're being generous. Keeping it a secret ensures that you know you're doing it not for yourself, but for others. And even though you don't get the buzz from people knowing what a great person you are, the fact that YOU know what a great person you are will make giving of your time ten times more valuable to you.

And if you've still got some "give" in you after all that, you can do even more. The Jewish Talmud recognizes eight different levels of giving. The highest level, the most noble, is not just to help somebody, but to help somebody to become self-sufficient. To invest the time to help them overcome not just their immediate challenges, but their long-term challenges, so that they can eventually stop needing help, and start helping others.

In other words, "Give a person a fish, and you feed them for a day. Teach a person to fish, and you feed them for a lifetime."

Admittedly, it's not easy to invest your time to selflessly help others. If you can spend even two hours a week (that's only 1 percent of your time) helping others, you're doing more than most people.

No matter how much time or money you spend, and no matter how you decide to do it, help somebody in some way. Give of yourself. And give more than you get. If you do that, you will inevitably get more than you expect.

"Helping others is the way we help ourselves."

–Oprah Winfrey

Help an Author
(And One Hundred Million Other People)

I hope you enjoyed reading *Dad's Great Advice: Top Ten Greatest Great Advice of All Time*, and more importantly, I hope the book was helpful to you! If it was, I hope you'll keep reading...

Years ago, I heard one of my all-time favorite pieces of Great Advice from author and speaker (and father of three) Shep Hyken, who insightfully said, "Every interaction you have is an opportunity to make a positive impact on others." Since then, I've made a real effort to put his Great Advice into effect with my children, friends, and everybody I meet, either through offering a piece of Great Advice, telling a "dad joke," or by putting a smile on somebody's face in some other way.

The *Dad's Great Advice* book series began as a way to make a positive impact on just four people. I wrote down all the Great Advice I had collected from parents and experts over the years and printed it in a book written solely for those four people: my children. But word of the book spread, the series quickly grew, and my Great Advice has now had a positive impact on thousands of people all over the world. Still, I wanted to do more.

Eventually, I made it my mission to try to make a positive impact on just 1% of the population. I figure if 100 other people try to do the same, then the whole world will be taken care of. With the world population at just around eight billion people (and rounding up for inflation), that means I only have to help about 100 million people. No problemo!

The *Dad's Great Advice* book series was born from this mission to help 100 million people. Specifically, my mission to "Have a positive impact on 100 million people with at least one piece of Great Advice that improves each person's life in a meaningful way."

If you've found at least one piece of Great Advice from this book helpful enough to improve your life in a meaningful way, then I'm one additional person closer to achieving that goal. And if so, would you please join me in my mission to help 100 million other people by spreading the word and sharing your favorite piece of Great Advice with one other person you know?

Or if you're busy and that takes too much time, can you simply spend fourteen seconds and one click of a button to leave a rating (from one to five) for this book right now by going to:

greatadvicegroup.com/review10

If you go the extra mile by not only leaving a rating but also leaving a short, one-sentence review of this book, you should know that I read each and every review written, so you have my sincere appreciation!

Thank you for taking the time to read this book. I sincerely hope you found my Great Advice to indeed be great, and I hope you're able to put some of it into action to improve your life in a meaningful way.

Best regards,

P.S. If you haven't done so already, make sure you get your free download of this book's *Challenge Checklist* here:

greatadvicegroup.com/checklist10

About the Author

Marc Fienberg spends his free time researching and talking to fellow dads, moms, scientists, psychologists, and experts, trying to learn as much Great Advice as possible to share with the world. He also happens to be an author, movie director, strategy consultant, entrepreneur, owner of The Great Advice Group, husband, father to four teenagers, and all-around nice guy. He has served as a life coach to his kids for almost two decades, and since none of them have been rushed to the emergency room or spent a night in jail yet, it seems like his Great Advice is working. To learn more about him, go to greatadvicegroup.com.

Other Dad's Great Advice Books available at greatadvicegroup.com

Dad's Great Advice for Teens

Dad's Great Advice for Parents of Teens

Dad's Great Advice for College Students

Dad's Great Advice for Everyone

Dad's Great Advice for All Parents

Dad's Great Advice About Life Skills for Teens

Printed in Great Britain
by Amazon

33179666R00059